GU00832890

Making a Newspaper

by Sarah Allen
illustrated by Chris Evans

Produced by Dinosaur Publications for
Cambridge University Press

Cambridge
London   New York   New Rochelle
Melbourne   Sydney

A lot of people don't know where
the news in their newspaper comes from,
or who writes it.

A boy's parents telephone the local paper
to say that their son has made and painted
over 100 model aeroplanes, and hopes to set up
an exhibition in their garage, to collect for charity.
Someone else knows a famous person
and writes to one of the national papers
to offer a story about him.

Reporters have a full-time job collecting news.
The local reporter goes to many different places,
including the courts, council meetings,
entertainments and sporting events.

On a big newspaper, each reporter usually
reports on a particular subject.
The political reporter will report
the latest debate in Parliament.
Someone else goes to the glittering fashion shows,
and a sports reporter writes about
an important tennis match.

Really big news, such as wars, earthquakes, or the
death of a world leader are usually on television and
radio first, but the newspaper reporter will have
gathered more details and writes much more of
the background story.

After going out to interview people and gather the facts, reporters write up their stories. They look for ways to interest their readers. Two reporters from different newspapers write about a strike at a factory. One writes about the angry workers preventing other people from getting on with their jobs, while another writes about the new machines which the workers fear will put many of them out of work.

A reporter goes out to cover a demonstration where there may be trouble.
She has two photographers with her.
One takes his pictures straight away and hurries back to develop them quickly for the next edition. The other one stays with the reporter, and helps to find out the details of what's happening.

The reporter may spend hours at one place, because lots of questions need to be asked, and it often takes a long time to make a story from the answers. A photographer can do his work more quickly and can visit many places in a day.

If there is a rush to get a story printed,
the reporter may phone it in.
The office typists wear special telephone headphones,
leaving their hands free to type as
the reporter dictates.

While newspapers report the happenings of the day, there are also many articles on other subjects to interest the readers. How to cut the cost of the family's weekly shopping bill; making model aeroplanes; articles on the United Nations; the private life of a top golfer; or child care, may be included.

The sports page covers sporting news with all the latest results. A few newspapers have nothing but sporting news. Many newspapers have cartoons, too — these may be the most popular thing in the paper!

The Chief Sub-Editor decides
which story will go on to the front page.
One newspaper fills its front page with a story about
an earthquake in South America – another chooses
the story of a rock star's new love affair.

Each page of the paper has to be marked out
so that the stories will fit the space. People put
advertisements in newspapers, and because these
have fixed sizes and shapes, they are measured out
on the page first. The news and the other stories
then have to be fitted into the rest of the space.
This is sometimes done by changing the
size of the type used to print the story,
or by altering the size or shape of photographs.

The sub-editors start fitting in feature articles
a day early – they try to have only the latest news
to fit in on publication day.

Each story then goes to the typesetters.
They type out the story and put it into the computer
which prints it out again ready to be checked.
The final version is printed out with the
words the right size to fit onto the newspaper page.

All the advertisements and the stories are
pasted onto a card like a newspaper page.
Now each page is passed through a laser machine –
this makes the printing plate.
The plate is washed with chemicals so that
the ink will stick to the words and pictures.

The plate is fitted round a cylinder on the printing machine, with rollers on one side, and the paper going through on the other. The huge reels of paper may go through three or four cylinders, and are printed on both sides at once. The paper moves through the printing machine amazingly fast. At the other end of the machine, the paper is folded up like a concertina, trimmed and folded in half – a finished newspaper.

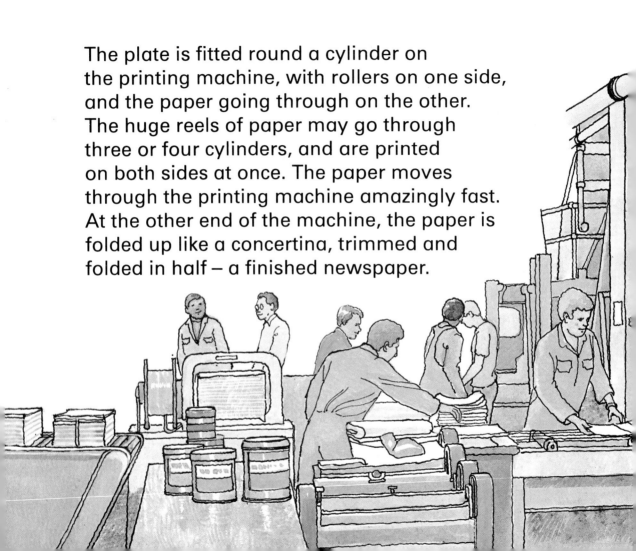

As soon as the papers are printed, they are rushed out to get to the shops on time. Some newspapers are sent all over the country, and they often go by train. There are also vans that deliver to all the newsagents.

Paperboys and papergirls deliver
a lot of the papers – they cycle or
walk around the streets taking the news
into people's houses.